Jazz Hanon

by Leo Alfassy

Jazz Hanon

by Leo Alfassy

Amsco Publications

New York/London/Sydney

Edited by Brenda Murphy
Cover illustration by Tom De Jong
Cover design by Werner Jurgeleit

Copyright © 1980 by Amsco Music Publishing Company,
A Division of Music Sales Corporation, New York, NY.

Order No. AM 27418
International Standard Book Number: 0.8256.2223.9

Exclusive Distributors:
Music Sales Corporation
257 Park Avenue South, New York, NY 10010 USA
Music Sales Limited
8/9 Frith Street, London W1V 5TZ England
Music Sales Pty. Limited
120 Rothschild Street, Rosebery, Sydney, NSW 2018, Australia

Printed in the United States of America by
Vicks Lithograph and Printing Corporation

Contents

Preface

Although there are many jazz piano books already available, the author feels that there is a pressing need for a manual which covers both the theorietical and the practical aspects of jazz piano in one comprehensive volume. Many young aspiring pianists, aware of the importance of basic theory for acquiring a good technique of improvisation, seek the essential information in theoretical books, but are soon turned off by the way the material is presented. Likewise, studies devoted exclusively to the development of a keyboard dexterity tend to be boring and discouraging.

This book does not pretend to cover all aspects which are necessary for a creative musical performance exhaustively. But each chapter deals with a specific technical problem thoroughly, followed by special exercises devoted to this problem. In addition, the idiomatic language and the stylistic features of the different schools of thought, from the end of ragtime to the beginning of "progressive" jazz, are discussed here.

The author hopes to enhance the awareness of the student that a rewarding musical experience depends greatly on the mastering of both the theoretical part and the basic techniques of playing jazz piano.

Introduction

Jazz is the most important contribution made by the American black to the art of music. It is a dynamic art form which has never remained stagnant—its history reveals a continuing process of evolution in which its personality has been steadily changing. At a very fast pace, in less than a hundred years, jazz underwent a similar evolution as music of the western world in about a thousand years—from the monophonic primitivism of Dixieland, to the homophonic texture of the big band era, and finally to the atonal and twelve-tone technique of the *avant-garde*. And in the same way, jazz is built on the four basic elements: melody, harmony, rhythm, and color. The basic difference between the so-called "serious" music and jazz lies in the two most characteristic features of jazz:

1. Unlike western concert music, it is not an exact reproduction of a written score; the performer plays melodic variations on a given harmonic sequence, thus becoming a composer in his own right. In other words, there is no clear distinction between composer and interpreter.
2. Jazz owes its idiosyncratic nature to the subtleties of its performing practices—the attack, the rhythmic pulse, the inflection, the vibrato, and all other expressive devices.

The history of jazz is intrinsically connected with a process of continuous harmonic exploration. Basically, its harmony is built on the same major and minor tonal system established during the baroque period (1600-1750). It is absolutely essential for every jazz musician to familiarize himself with the rudiments of traditional harmony in order to be able to accompany a singer or another musician, to harmonize a melody, or to improvise.

Elements of Jazz Harmony

Intervals and Triads

Melody and harmony are two aspects of the same building material, the *interval*. Intervals represent the distance in pitch between two tones. A melody is a horizontal succession of intervals, while harmony is a vertical superposition of intervals. The name of each interval indicates the total number of tones between the lowest note (the root) and the highest note.

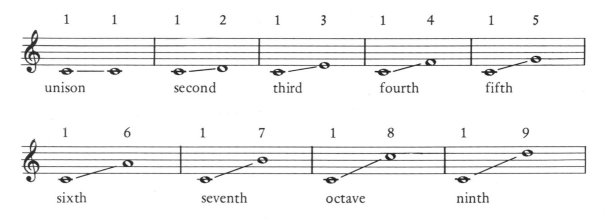

The simplest chords are the triads built of two superposed thirds.

Each of the seven degrees of the major and minor scales can be the root of a triad.

scale degrees

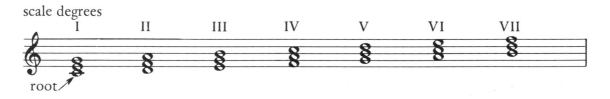

The triads on the I, IV, and V degrees, the "tonal" degrees, are the most important in each scale and occur more frequently than the other four degrees (II, III, VI, VII), Any tone of any chord can be sharped or flatted, *i.e.* it can be raised or lowered by a half step (semitone). Thus, a major triad can be transformed into a minor one by flatting the third, or vice versa. If we also flat the fifth, the minor chord becomes a diminished triad. If the fifth of a major chord is raised it becomes an augmented triad.

The triads on the "tonal" degrees (I, IV, and V) in a major scale, are always major (M); the triads on the II, III, and VI degrees are minor (m). Only the triad on the VII degree is diminished (°) because it consists of two superposed minor thirds.

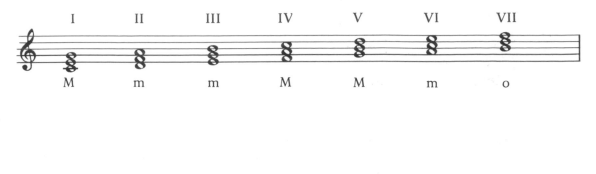

Seventhis

Simple triads are used sparingly in jazz. To add color and excitement to the music, more complicated chordal structures are utilized, such as seventh chords and triads with added note(s).

Seventh chords are triads with still another third superposed.

The most common triad with an added note in jazz is the triad with an added sixth.

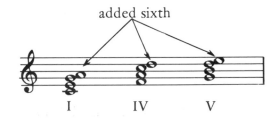

Each of the seven degrees of the major and minor scales can be the root of a seventh chord. Here are the scale-tone seventh chords in C major.

The seventh chords built on the I and IV degrees are *major seventh chords* (M7) because they consist of a major triad and a major seventh (the major seventh is located a half step below the octave).

The seventh chords built on the II, III, and VI degrees are *minor seventh chords* (m7) because they consist of a minor triad and a minor seventh (the minor seventh is located a whole step below the octave).

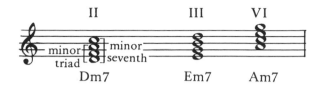

The seventh chord on V is called the *dominant seventh chord* (7) because the V degree of the scale is the "dominant." It consists of a major triad and a minor seventh. The seventh chord on VII is a *half-diminished seventh chord* (∅) because it consists of a diminished triad and a minor seventh. By lowering the seventh of a half-diminished chord (in this case from A to A♭) we obtain a *diminished seventh chord* (o), which consists of three superposed minor thirds.

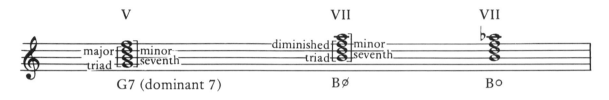

Seventh Chords

The first exercises explore seventh chords and triads with added sixth in both hands; in the left hand they are arranged vertically (harmonic), in the right hand horizontally (melodic). As you will notice, the first exercise is provided with chord symbols below the staff and figured bass above it. The *figured bass*, one of the major contributions of the baroque period to the development of our musical language, is by far more precise than chord letters. It is regrettable that it is still not adopted by jazz musicians and music publishers, although some jazz theorists made an attempt to popularize it some twenty years ago. For that reason, this book will utilize chord symbols.

These first exercises also introduce the student to the three basic rhythmic units in jazz: the eighth note, the eighth-note triplet, and the sixteenth note. When playing the exercises carefully note that the common performance practice in jazz is to play the ♪♩ or the ♩. ♪ rhythm as ♪♪♪. The strongly syncopated figure ♪♩ ♪♩ what softened by interpreting it as ♪♪♪♩

Triads and Seventh Chords

1

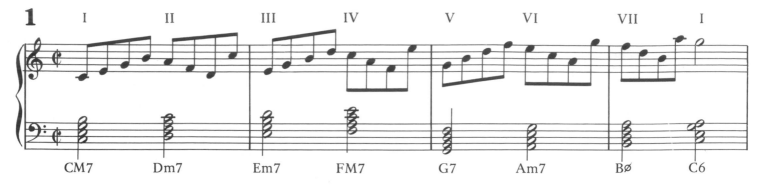

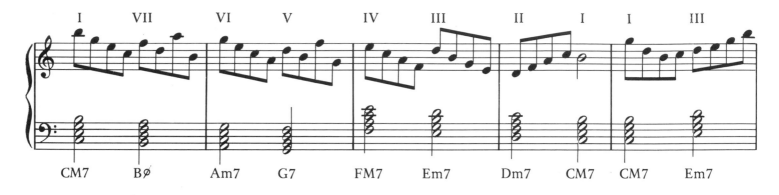

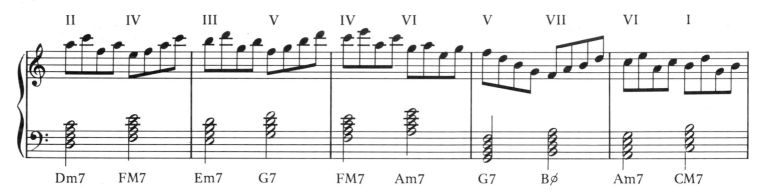

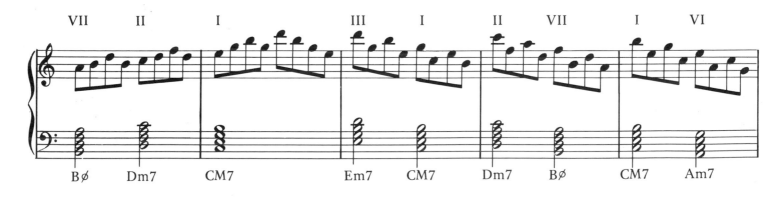

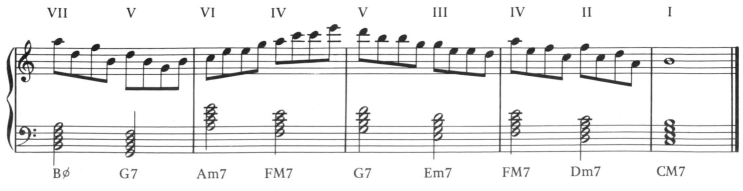

2

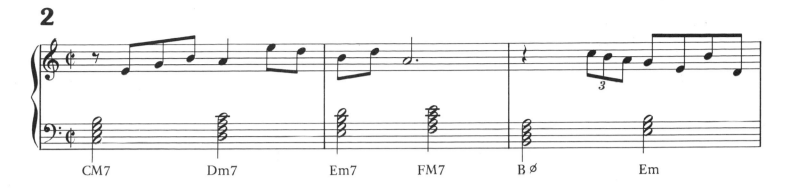

CM7   Dm7   Em7   FM7   B∅   Em

Am7   FM7   Dm7   B∅   Em7   Am7

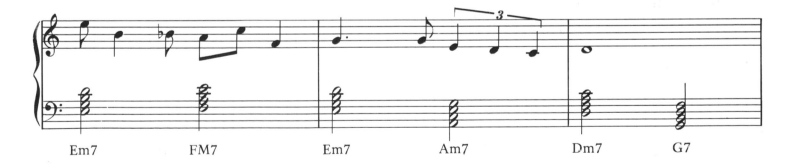

FM7   Em7   Dm7   B∅   C6   CM7   Em7   C6   CM7   Dm7

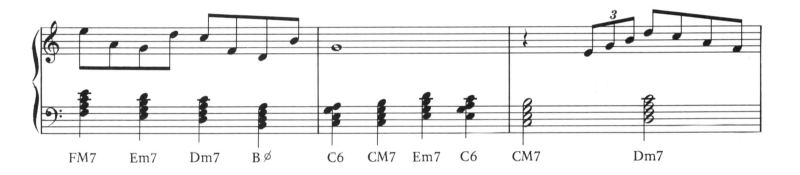

Em7   FM7   Em7   Am7   Dm7   G7

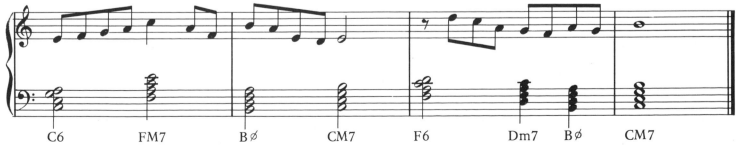

C6   FM7   B∅   CM7   F6   Dm7   B∅   CM7

3

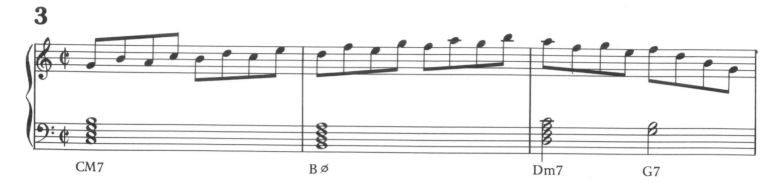

CM7   B ⌀   Dm7   G7

CM7   F   B ⌀   Em   Am7   B ⌀   CM7   Dm7

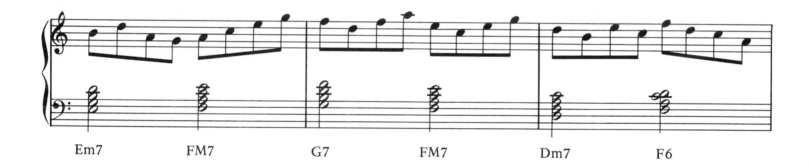

Em7   FM7   G7   FM7   Dm7   F6

Dm7   C6   B ⌀   CM7

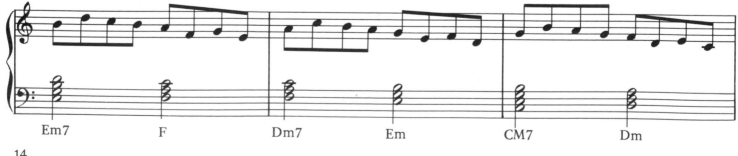

Em7   F   Dm7   Em   CM7   Dm

G7   Am7   Bø   CM7   Dm7   Em7

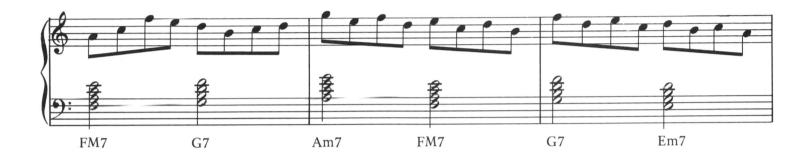

FM7   G7   Am7   FM7   G7   Em7

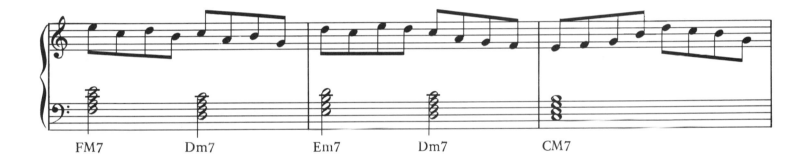

FM7   Dm7   Em7   Dm7   CM7

Dm7   Em7   FM7

G7   C6   Bø   C6

4

CM7   Dm7   Em7

FM7   G7   FM7

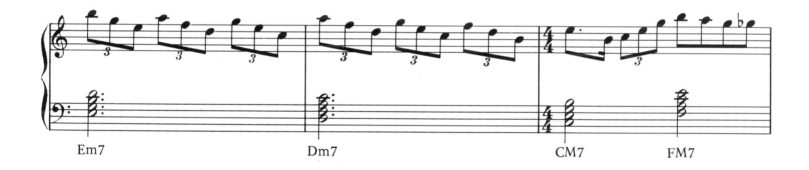

Em7   Dm7   CM7   FM7

Dm7   G7   Em7   Am7   FM7   Bø

Em7   Am   Dm7   G   CM7   F

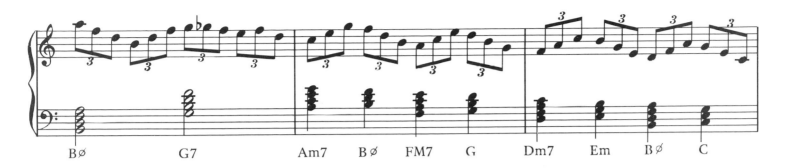

B∅ G7   Am7 B∅ FM7 G Dm7 Em B∅ C

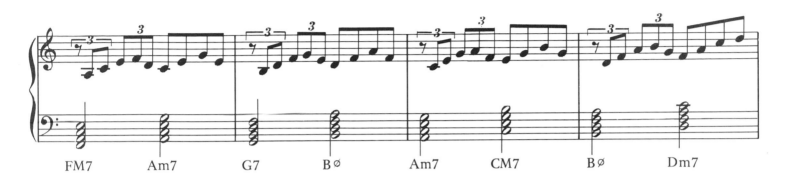

FM7 Am7 G7 B∅ Am7 CM7 B∅ Dm7

FM7   Em7   Dm7

CM7   Dm7   Em7   FM7

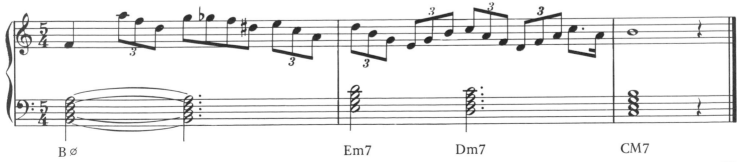

B∅   Em7 Dm7   CM7

5

CM7   Dm7   Em7   FM7

G7   Am7   B⌀   C6   Am7

Dm7   G7   Em7

Am7   FM7   B⌀

G7   C6   FM7

B ∅   Em7   Am7

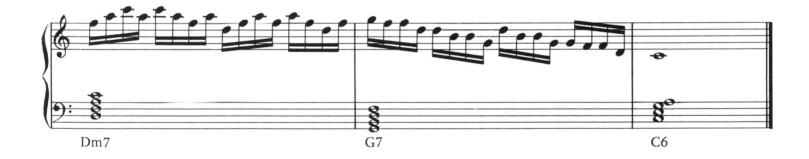

Dm7   G7   C6

Simplified Seventh Chords

Modern pianists create interesting sonorities by selecting and rearranging certain notes of a chord and omitting others. This device, called *voicing*, originated in the 1940s, when the famous pianist Bud Powell replaced the old fashioned "oom-pah" left-hand accompaniment with half-note seventh chords consisting of the root and the seventh only. It is essential that the right-hand improvisations contain these missing notes, because the interval of a seventh can only "suggest" the quality of a complete seventh chord. As you can see from the next example, the seventh C-Bb can stand for either a dominant, minor, or half-diminished seventh chord.

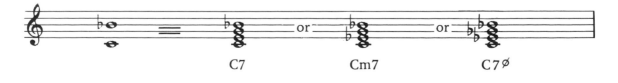

C7   Cm7   C7∅

6

Dm7 G7 CM7 FM7 B∅ Em7

Am7 Dm7 G7   C7

F7   Bb 7   Eb 7

Ab 7   C   Bb

Ab   G   FM7 F6

Gm7   Gm6   Am7   F   B♭M7   B♭6   C7

C○   Bø   B○   CM7

Am7   FM7   Dm7   G7

G#○   Am7   A#○   Bø   E7

Am7   D7   Dm7   G7   CM7

7

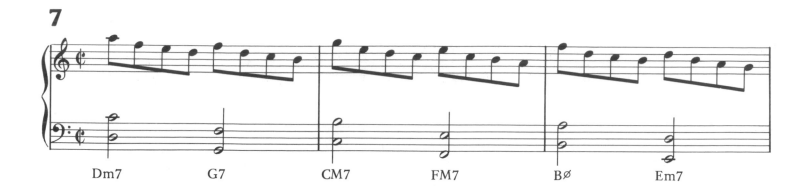

Dm7   G7   CM7   FM7   Bø   Em7

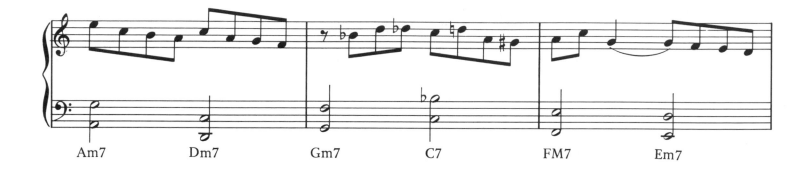

Am7   Dm7   Gm7   C7   FM7   Em7

AM7   Bm7   C♯m7   DM7   Em7   Am7

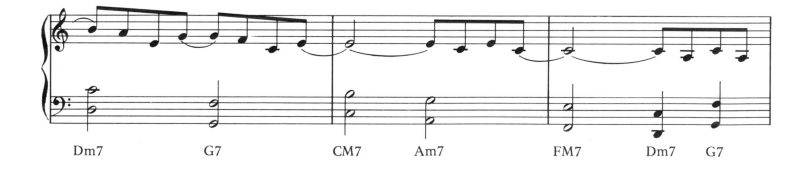

Dm7   G7   CM7   Am7   FM7   Dm7   G7

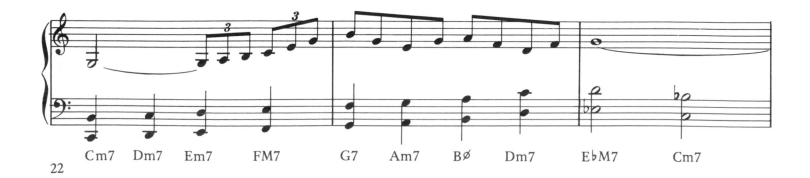

Cm7 Dm7 Em7   FM7   G7 Am7 Bø Dm7   E♭M7   Cm7

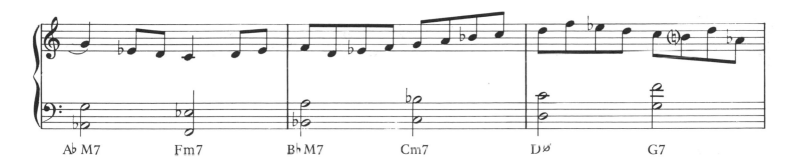

A♭ M7   Fm7   B♭ M7   Cm7   D∅   G7

CM7   Dm7   Em7   FM7

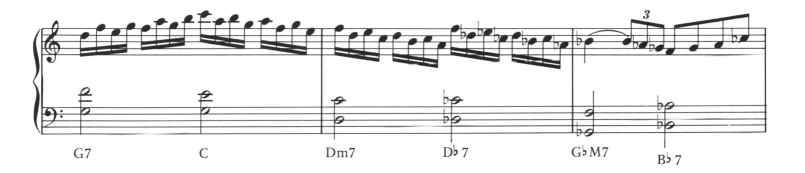

G7   C   Dm7   D♭ 7   G♭ M7   B♭ 7

F♭ M7   G7   CM7   FM7   B∅   Em7

Am7   Dm7   G7   FM7   Em7   Dm7   CM7

Walking Bass

One of the oldest bass patterns in jazz piano is the walking bass. This is a bass line that "walks" up and down a scale or in broken chords. This left-hand pattern was taken over from the bass player whose assignment in the band is to sustain the basic metric unit in jazz—the quarter note. The monotony of the walking bass can be avoided by replacing some quarter notes with the ♩♪ figure—a device commonly used by modern bass players. This figure falls mostly on the second and the fourth beats of the measure.

The bass line in the next two exercises consist entirely of walking basses. The melodic lines explore all kinds of durations and rhythmic figures.

8

C6   F7   C

C7   F7

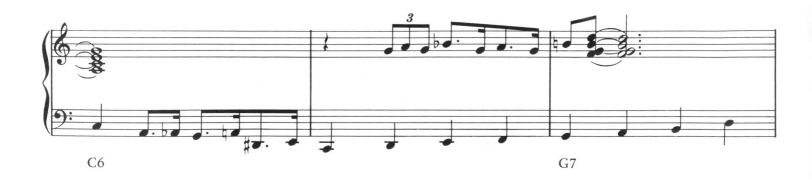

C6   G7

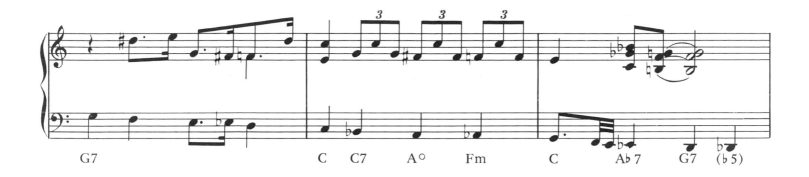

G7 C C7 A° Fm C A♭7 G7 (♭5)

C6 F7 C6

C7 F7

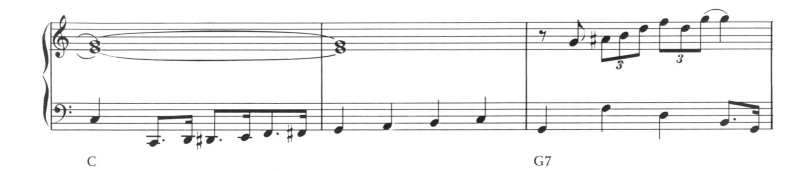

C G7

F7 C C7 F A♭7 C D♭7 C7

9

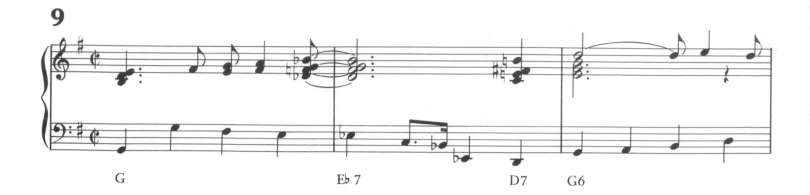

G   E♭7   D7   G6

E7   Am7   D7   D♯○

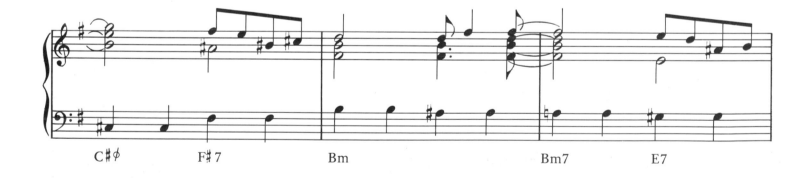

Em   B7   Em7

C♯⌀   F♯7   Bm   Bm7   E7

A   AM7   DM7   GM7   CM7

FM7   B7   Em7   A7   DM7   D7

G   G#°   D   Eb

D   D#ø   D#°   Em7   A7   Am7   D7

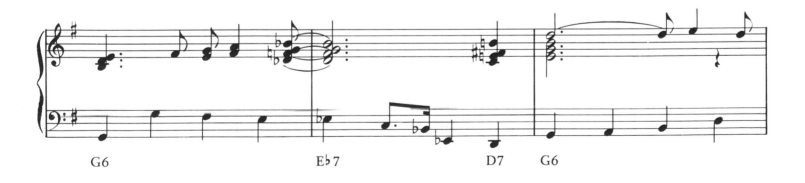

G6   Eb7   D7   G6

Inversions

The preceding exercises dealt mainly with triads and seventh chords in root position. Any chord is said to be in *root position* as long as the root remains the lowest note, regardless of the position of the other notes.

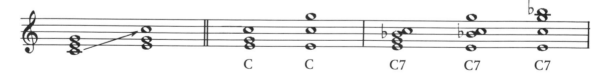

If we move the root one octave higher so that the third (in this example the E) lies in the bass, then the chord is said to be in *first inversion*.

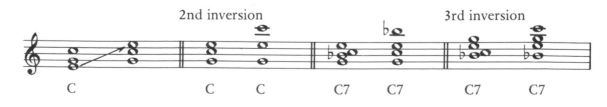

If the fifth (the G in a C major chord) is in the bass, the chord is in *second inversion*. If the seventh of a seventh chord is in the bass, it is in *third inversion*.

Jazz music is dominated mostly by chords in root position, but inversions are used increasingly by modern pianists.

10

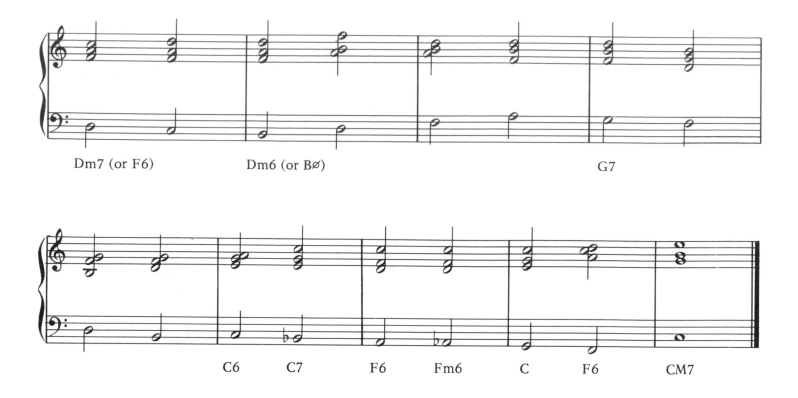

Dm7 (or F6)   Dm6 (or B∅)   G7

C6   C7   F6   Fm6   C   F6   CM7

*Notice that this chord can be interpreted as a C6 or as the first inversion of an Am7 chord.

Rule: Any triad with an added sixth is the same as the first inversion of a seventh chord with the root a minor third below.

C6 = first inversion of Am7
Dm6 = first inversion of B∅
G6 = first inversion of Em7, etc.

Only the diminished seventh chord is said to be always in root position because it consists of three superposed thirds which divide the octave into four equal intervals. Thus, each member of a diminished seventh chord can become the root.

equal intervals:
minor third

11

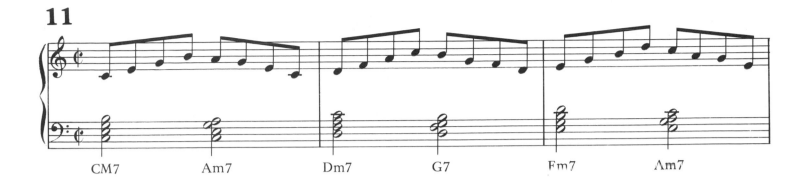

CM7   Am7   Dm7   G7   Fm7   Am7

FM7   Bø   E7   Am6   Dm7   D°

Em7   CM7   Bø   E7   Am7   Dm

G7   C6   Cm6   G7   CM7   C7

FM7   Bø   Em7   Am7   Dm7   G7

C7   F   Bø   E7   Am7   D7

Bb C7   FM7 C○   B○ G7   C7 F7

G#○   G7   C   Am7   Dm   G7

C7   A○   G#○ A7   D7   Bø

CM7 C7   F6   Fm6   G7 Bb○ D7 G7 C6

Circle of Fifths

The circle of fifths always has played a preponderant role in jazz harmony. This design is not new; it was first described in 1728 in a German theoretical book, but had already been applied in seventeenth-century compositions.

The circle of fifths is a circular arrangement of the twelve keys in such a way that the number of sharps in the key signature increases clockwise, and the number of flats counterclockwise. After twelve steps the initial key is reached again. The same principle is valid for the minor keys, but the starting point is from A instead of from C.

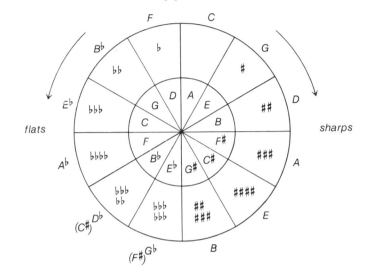

Every musical composition consists of harmonic progressions arranged in a certain way. Jazz uses primarily patterns based on the circle of fifths in a counterclockwise direction. In other words, the C chord is followed by the F chord situated a fifth lower (or a fourth higher), followed by B♭, etc. The next example shows this design.

The same design can be arranged in a more practical way, *i.e.* moving from the C a fifth down to F, then a fourth up to B♭, then down again, etc.

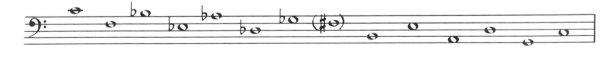

In this way the design is squeezed within a narrow area of the keyboard easily reached by the left hand. But it becomes almost impossible to play when chords are added to each root. Parallel dominant seventh chords built on the circle of fifths look like this.

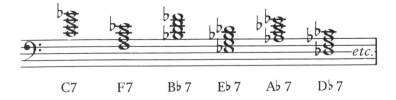

C7　　F7　　B♭7　　E♭7　　A♭7　　D♭7

By playing alternately the root and the seventh of one chord and the root and the third of the following chord this progression is simplified. Beginning with the minor seventh on C7, the circle of fifths can be played this way.

| C7 | F7 | Bb7 | Eb7 | Ab7 | Db7 | Gb7 | B7 | E7 | A7 | D7 | G7 |

If we begin with a third instead of a seventh, then we arrive at the following design.

| C7 | F7 | Bb7 | Eb7 | Ab7 | Db7 | Gb7 | B7 | E7 | A7 | D7 | G7 |

Note that in both examples the top voice moves downward chromatically, *i.e.* by half steps.

It is of the utmost importance to memorize these patterns which appear frequently in jazz tunes.

12

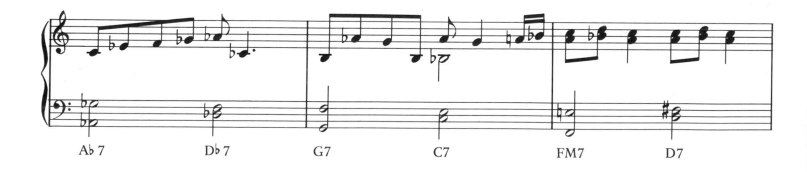

| C7 | F7 | C7 | F7 | Bb7 | Eb7 |

| Ab7 | Db7 | G7 | C7 | FM7 | D7 |

| Ab7 | Db7 | F | B7 | Bø | E7 |

A7   D7   GM7

G6   C7   F7   Bb7   Eb7

C#o   Am6   C   Gm7   Am7   BbM7

Cm7   Co   Bo   Bbo   D7   GM7   G6

C7   Co   Bo   Bbo   Am7   D7

Dm7   G7   CM7 Dm7 Em7 E♭7   Dm7   G7   C7   F7

B♭7   E♭7   A♭7   D♭7   G♭7   B7   E7   A7

D7   G7   CM7   .C6

Chromatic Alterations

Each scale tone can be altered chromatically by raising or lowering it by a semitone (half step). A note preceded by a sharp or a flat is an indication that this particular note has been altered. For instance, the symbol (♭5) under a chord means that the fifth of the chord has been flatted; the symbol (♯5) means that the fifth has been sharped.

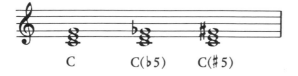

C   C(♭5)   C(♯5)

The augmented fifth (♯5) is often indicated by a plus sign (+). If two or more notes of a chord are altered, then each note is preceded by a sharp or flat. A ninth chord with an augmented fifth and a flat ninth is indicated this way.

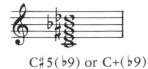

C♯5(♭9) or C+(♭9)

Sometimes a note is momentarily *suspended* or replaced by another note. The 4-3 suspension is the one most frequently found in scores; it is marked as "sus 4."

C sus 4   C

By sharping or flatting one or more notes of a chord we obtain altered chords. The most common altered chords are those built on the II, IV, V, and VI degrees of the scale. Thus, through various alterations of one or more constituents, we obtain the following chords built on these degrees.

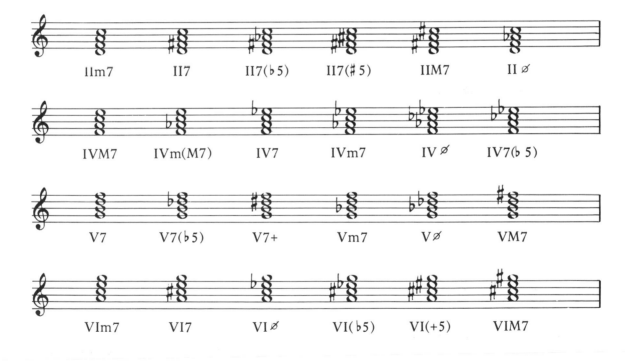

IIm7   II7   II7(♭5)   II7(♯5)   IIM7   II ∅

IVM7   IVm(M7)   IV7   IVm7   IV ∅   IV7(♭5)

V7   V7(♭5)   V7+   Vm7   V ∅   VM7

VIm7   VI7   VI ∅   VI(♭5)   VI(+5)   VIM7

The altered dominant seventh chord and its derivations (the ninth, eleventh, and thirteenth chords discussed in the next chapter) are most commonly used in jazz.

Sometimes all the notes of a chord are raised or lowered chromatically, so that the whole chord is virtually transposed a semitone higher or lower.

II7   ♯II7   II7   or   VII∅   ♭VII∅

Chromatic notes are not only essential in creating interesting harmonic support; they can also enrich the melodic invention considerably. It is obvious that the monotony of a melody moving up and down the scale or in broken chords can be avoided by the use of chromatic tones. Here is the simplest way of doing it:

Before playing the notes of a triad or a seventh chord, first substitute these notes with their neighboring note below or above, and *then* play the essential notes. For instance, the essential notes of the C major triad are C E G. Before playing the E (or the E and the G), we can play the notes immediately below or above.

Chromatic notes can also be used to fill in the space between two notes:

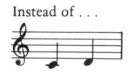

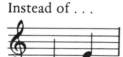

13

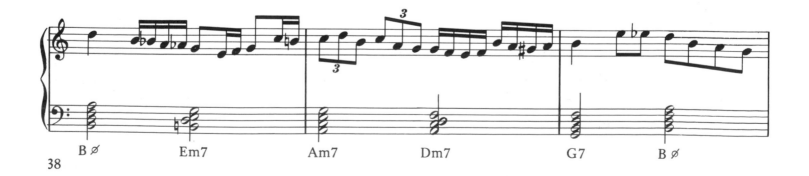

C7 C#° Dm7 G7 CM7 FM7

Bⵁ B♭7 B♭m7 E♭7 A♭M7 A♭6

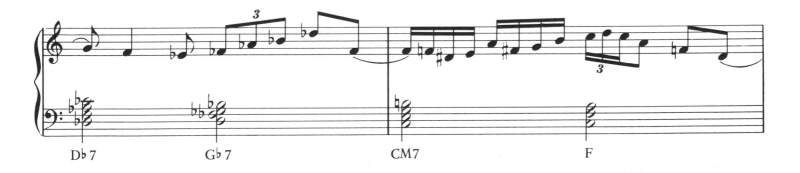

G7 C7 F7 B♭7 E♭7 A♭7

D♭7 G♭7 CM7 F

B♭M7 E♭6 A♭7 A♭6 A♭ G7 G6 G

B7 E7   A7 D7   G7 C7

FM7   D7   B7

G7(♭5) Gm7 G○ FM7 D7

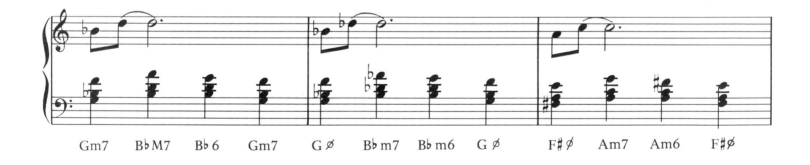

Gm7 B♭M7 B♭6 Gm7 Gø B♭m7 B♭m6 Gø F#ø Am7 Am6 F#ø

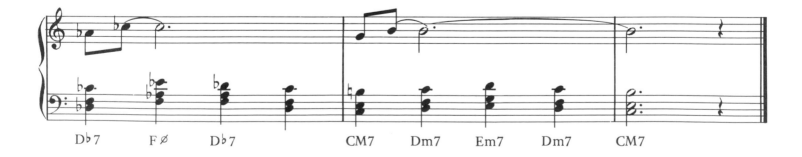

D♭7 F ø D♭7 CM7 Dm7 Em7 Dm7 CM7

Derivations of the Seventh Chord

The Ninth Chord

In the preceding chapters we explored the fundamental harmonic system of western music, namely the so-called tertian harmony. In this system, chords are built by super-position of thirds: a triad consists of two superposed thirds, a seventh chord consists of three. To achieve more variety and color, more complicated harmonies can be created by superposing additional thirds on the seventh chord. A chord that consists of a third, fifth, seventh, and ninth above the root is called a ninth chord (9).

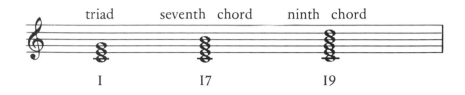

The ninth can be superposed on the five types of seventh chords we already know: the major, the dominant, the minor, the half-diminished, and the diminished seventh chords.

By adding the major or minor (flat) ninth to the root of these seventh chords, we can obtain the following ninth chords.

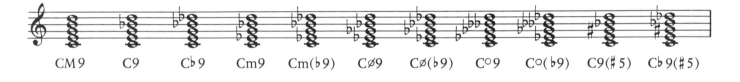

The most frequently-used ninth chords are those built on the dominant seventh chord, *i.e.* the *dominant ninth* and the *dominant flat ninth chord*.

A chord often found in sheet music is the major triad with *added sixth and ninth* ($^6_9$) which sounds best in the following two positions.

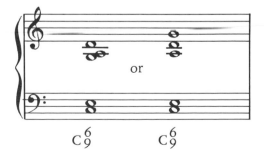

Another chord used frequently in jazz since the 1920s is the so-called *augmented ninth chord*. This chord gives the illusion of containing a major and a minor third simultaneously. Actually, the augmented ninth can be interpreted as an unresolved appoggiatura of a flat ninth chord.

This chord is always used in root position and without the fifth, G.

It is extremely difficult to play a complete ninth chord with one hand. For that reason, one or two of its constituents are omitted, usually the root and/or the fifth.

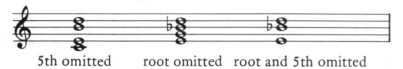

Note that the ninth with the root omitted sounds exactly like a half-diminished seventh chord. It can be interpreted as the seventh chord of the seventh degree of the scale (VII⌀).

In traditional harmony, the ninth chord was used sparingly and only in root position—the ninth had to be in the upper voice, and the two upper voices were not allowed to form a second. Jazz musicians are not preoccupied with these outdated rules. On the contrary, the history of jazz is intrinsically connected with the search for a richer harmonic vocabulary. The *avant-garde* musicians of today went beyond the realm of tertian harmony, exploring quartal harmony, atonality, and dodecaphonism.

Inversions of the ninth chord are obtained in the same way as triads and seventh chords—by moving each constituent an octave higher consecutively.

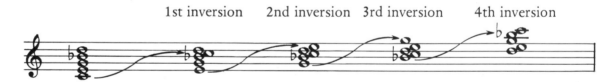

14

G9   Gm9

C9   Gm6   F9

F(♭9)   E♭9   D♭9

D(♯9)   Gm9   Gø9

B♭9   D9   E9

E(♭9)   A9   C9

C(♭9)   E♭(♭9)   D9

B9   A♭9   C(♯9)

F9   DM9   DØ9

D○9   D♭(♯9)   E♭(♭9)

Dm9   G9 C^{6}_{9} G9

FM9 E9   A9 Aⱷ9   D9 D(♭9)

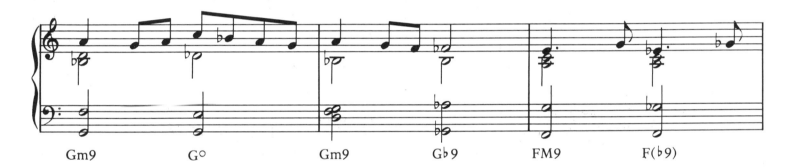

Gm9 G°   Gm9 G♭9   FM9 F(♭9)

B♭9 B♭(♭9) E♭9 A♭9 A♭(♭9) DM9

EM9   AM9 Aⱷ9   A♭9 D♭9

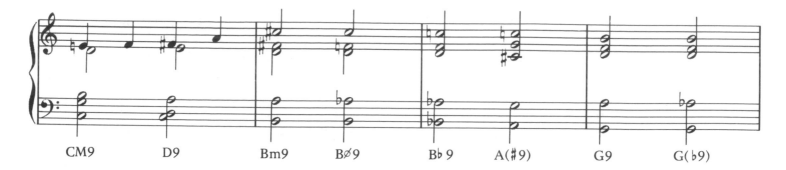

CM9   D9   Bm9   B∅9   B♭9   A(♯9)   G9   G(♭9)

G♭9   C9   FM9   F(♭9)   B♭9   E♭9

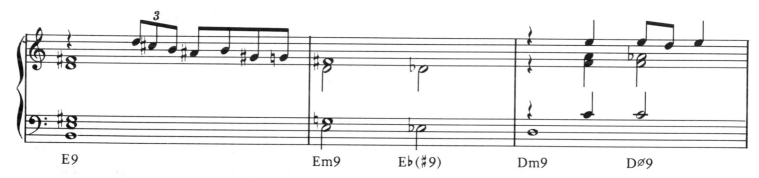

E9   Em9   E♭(♯9)   Dm9   D∅9

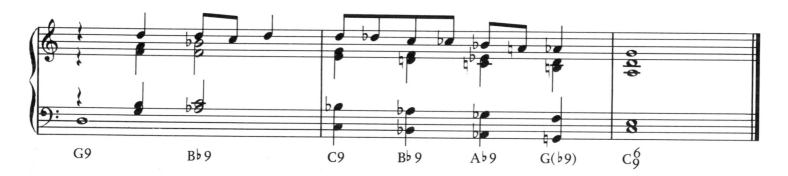

G9   B♭9   C9   B♭9   A♭9   G(♭9)   C$\frac{6}{9}$

Eleventh and Thirteenth Chords

By superposing another minor or major third on the ninth chord we obtain the *eleventh* and the *augmented eleventh chord*.

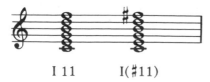

I 11   I(♯11)

The augmented eleventh (F♯) is actually a diminished fifth (C-G♭). Many eleventh chord combinations are possible, but some of them are avoided because of their dissonant quality. Furthermore, many are cumbersome and require the omission of one or more constituents.

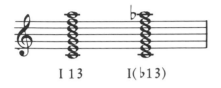

CM(♯11)　　C11　　Cm11　　Cø11　　C○11

Thirteenth chords are created by the superposition of another major or minor third on the eleventh chord.

I 13　　I(♭13)

It is obvous that the more notes we add to a chord structure, the more cumbersome and unplayable it becomes. The inversions become also more and more dissonant because of the closeness of major and minor seconds. For that reason and in order to gain clarity, the unessential notes of the chord are often omitted.

The next example shows various types of eleventh and thirteenth chords with omitted notes.

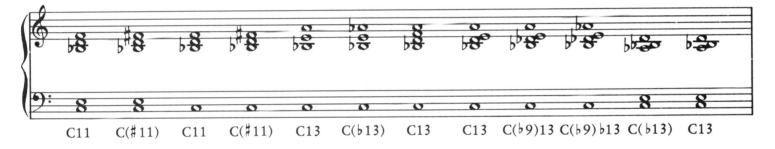

C11　C(♯11)　C11　C(♯11)　C13　C(♭13)　C13　C13　C(♭9)13　C(♭9)♭13　C(♭13)　C13

15

C9　　　　　　　　F13　　　　　　　　Bb 9　　　　　　　Bb 13

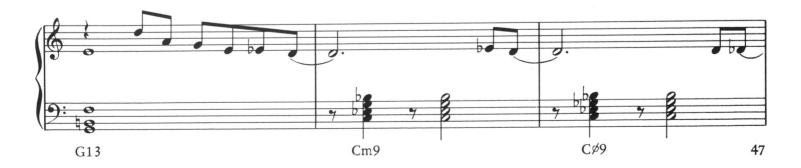

G13　　　　　　　　Cm9　　　　　　　　Cø9

F(♭13)   G11   C(♯9)   C13

F6/9   Fm11   E9(♭5)   A(♭9)♭13   D(♭13)   G(♯9)   C(♯11)

A13   D(♯9)   G13   D♭(♭13)   C9   Cm9

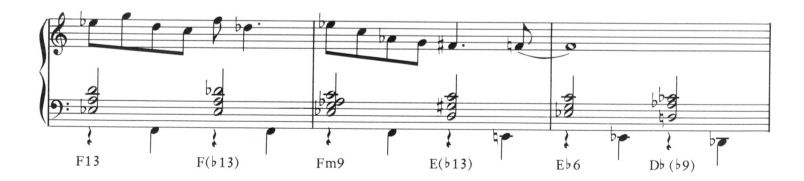

F13   F(♭13)   Fm9   E(♭13)   E♭6   D♭(♭9)

C7   B(♭9)   F♯13   F13

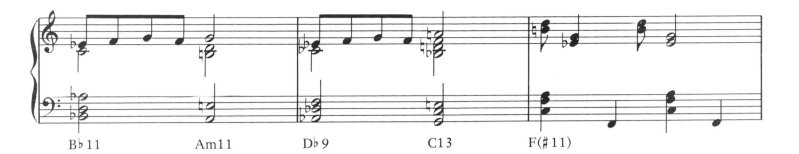

Bb11   Am11   Db9   C13   F(#11)

Gb(#11)   G(#11) Gb(#11) F(#11) E(#11) Eb(#11)

D13   CM(#11)   Am11   F(#11)   Dm11   Db9   C$^6_9$

Substitution Chords

Every triad containing two notes in common with another triad can be used as its substitution.

As we can see from the above example, the root of the substitution chord lies a third above or below that of the original chord. The same rule can be applied to seventh chords, in which case the two chords must have three notes in common.

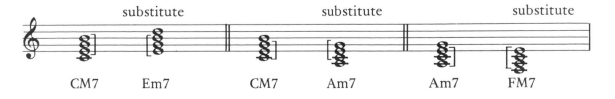

Actually, the substitution chord with the root a third above the original chord can be interpreted as a ninth chord without a root (Em7=CM9 without root).

A frequently-used substitution chord for any dominant seventh chord is another dominant seventh chord whose root lies an augmented fourth (or diminished fifth) below. Thus, Db 7 can be substituted for G7, although in their unaltered form they have only two notes in common.

G7   Db 7

If we flat the fifth of both chords, then we obtain two identical chords, although with different spellings.

G7(b 5)   Db 7(b 5)

16

GM7   Em7   CM7

Am7   A ∅   A o

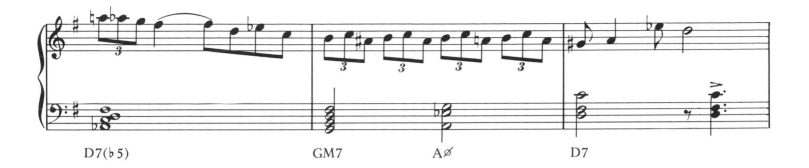

D7(b5)   GM7 A⌀   D7

G7   B7(b5) E 7   E⌀   Eb7

D6   DM7 Bm7   B⌀   CM7   Dm7

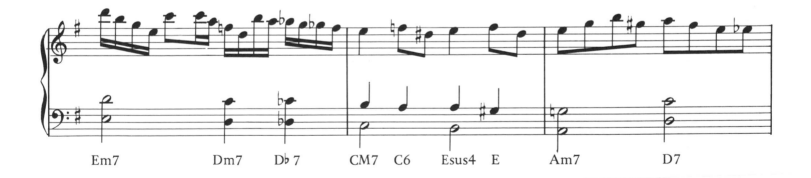

Em7   Dm7 Db7 CM7 C6 Esus4 E Am7   D7

Dm7   G7   C7   A7   Am9   F(#11)

D(♭9)13   B(♭9)13   Bø   G7

C   CM7   C6   Bø   E7   A7

A♭9   D♭13   E7(♭5)   E♭7   D7   A♭7   GM7   G6

II-V-I Progressions

All compositions contain certain harmonic progressions called *cadences* which occur at the end of a section or a phrase. A cadence conveys more or less the impression of momentary conclusion, depending on the kind of cadence and where it occurs. Before 1600, the most common cadential formula in music, especially in Gregorian chant, was the descending motion II-I, which was then replaced after the seventeenth century by the II-V-I progression.

The frequent use of this formula in classical and in popular music is due to the fact that the roots of these chords are a fifth apart, which results in very strong harmonic progressions. (See the chapter on the circle of fifths.) Jazz musicians achieved an amplification and embellishment of this simple design by introducing all kinds of ninth, eleventh, and thirteenth chords in the II-V-I progression.

The examples below show first the simplest II-V-I progressions followed by more complicated harmonic structures. Play the examples as written, then transpose them into the remaining eleven keys.

C major

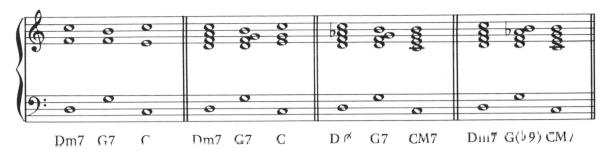

Dm7 G7 C   Dm7 G7 C   D⌀ G7 CM7   Dm7 G(♭9) CM7

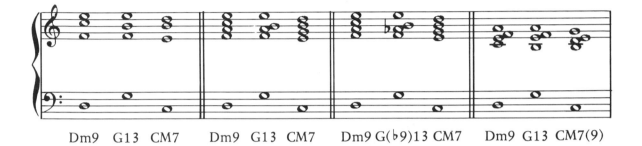

Dm9 G13 CM7   Dm9 G13 CM7   Dm9 G(♭9)13 CM7   Dm9 G13 CM7(9)

C minor

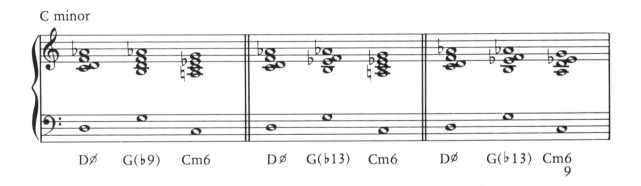

D⌀ G(♭9) Cm6   D⌀ G(♭13) Cm6   D⌀ G(♭13) Cm6
9

17

Gm7   C9   FM7   B♭M7   E∅   A(♭9)

DM7   B♭9   B♭m7   E♭(♭9)13   A♭M7   D♭(♯11)

Gm7   G♭7   FM7   Cm7

F7   B♭   Cm7   B7   B♭6   B♭M7

B♭m7   E♭7   A♭M7   D♭(♯11)   Gm7   C7

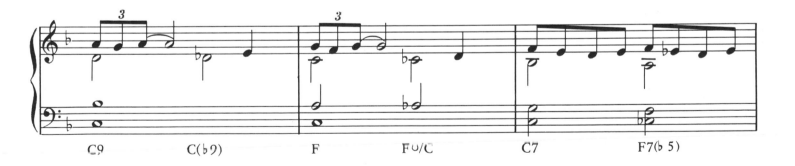

Harmonic Patterns

We have already discovered that the progressions following the circle of fifths counter-clockwise are the strongest. Thus, the harmonic progressions from one chord to another whose root is a fifth lower is a strong one and one which is most commonly used in classical and jazz music. Next strongest is the progression to a chord with root a third lower. Jazz musicians also often use another harmonic pattern—descending or ascending scale progressions. The pattern I-II-III-IV is a diatonic ascending pattern because the roots of these chords succeed each other on the scale. If the chords move up or down by half steps, then we obtain a chromatic pattern. Frequently-used chromatic patterns are:

III-♭ III-II-♭ II-I

II-♭ II-I

I-♯ I-II-♯ II-III

A diatonic pattern can sometimes be interrupted by a chromatic progression, resulting in a mixed pattern.

I-II-♭ III-III or

III-II-♭ II-I

18

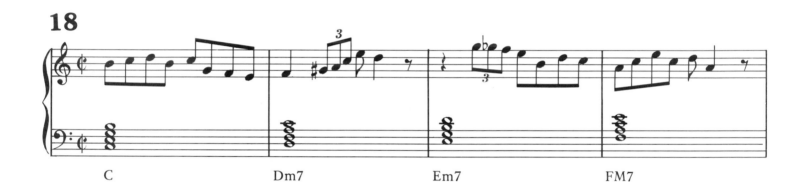

F6   FM7   C m7   D+(♯11)

E♭ m7   F+(♯11)   E7   E♭ 7

D7   D♭ 7   C7 sus4   C7   F6   B○

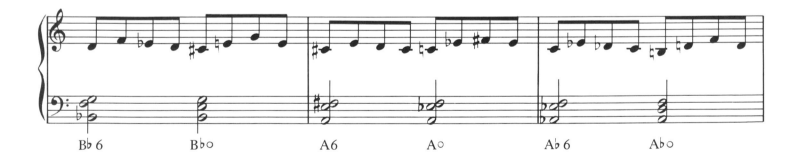

B♭ 6   B♭○   A6   A○   A♭ 6   A♭○

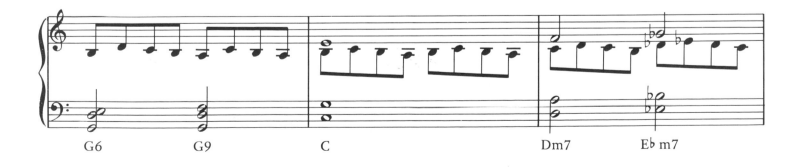

G6   G9   C   Dm7   E♭ m7

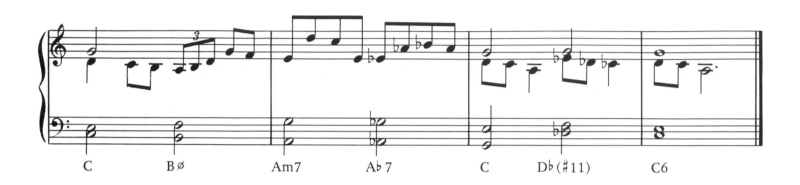

Scales and Modes

Modern jazz musicians try more and more to expand their harmonic vocabulary by exploring unusual scales and modes. This chapter deals with three of them: the whole tone, pentatonic, and blues scales.

The *whole-tone scale* consists of six whole tones equally spaced. In can be derived in the following way: by superposing an augmented triad over another augmented triad with the root a whole step above, we create a tone cluster containing the six notes of the whole-tone scale.

This scale can also be derived from an augmented dominant eleventh chord with augmented fifth, whose constituents succeed each other in stepwise motion.

There are only two whole-tone scales, built on C and on C♯ ; the others are only transpositions of these two scales.

on C   on C♯

Because of the lack of semitones, any one of its notes can be considered the tonic of a new scale. The notes can be arranged vertically in different ways, thus creating interesting harmonies.

These evanescent harmonies convey the atmosphere of vagueness, enchantment, haziness, but their prolonged use can also create monotony.

The *pentatonic scale* is another scale used both in modern music and in jazz, although a considerable number of Gregorian chants are pentatonic, as well as many melodies of ancient cultures (China, Japan, Africa, etc.). The pentatonic scale is sometimes called a "gapped" scale because it contains only five tones to the octave, creating gaps in the scale.

There are two basic pentatonic scales: with or without semitones. The scale which does not contain semitones is called *tonal pentatonic scale*. We can derive two varieties from this type of scale: one built on the major, the other built on the minor scale.

major   minor

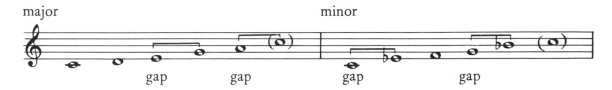

gap   gap   gap   gap

By starting each time from a different note on the scale we obtain the following five modes.

major tonal pentatonic scale

mode 1   mode 2   mode 3   mode 4   mode 5

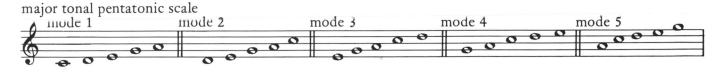

minor tonal pentatonic scale

mode 1   mode 2   mode 3   mode 4   mode 5

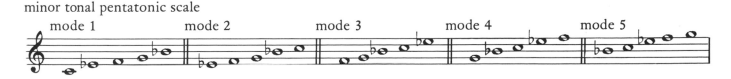

59

The *semitonal pentatonic scale* contains semitones by omitting the second and the sixth (a), or the second and the fifth degrees of the scale (b).

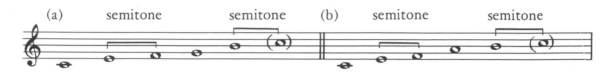

Five modes can be derived from these two scales in the same way as from the tonal pentatonic scale.

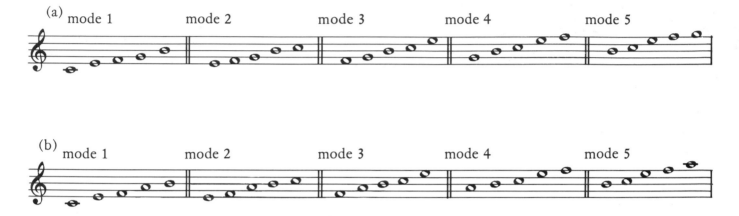

The blues contains a very characteristic feature, namely the so-called "blue" notes. These are notes (particularly the third, fifth, and seventh degrees of the scale) whose intonation lies between the major and the minor pitches. Our notational system is not apt to notate correctly these subtle intonations; in the score they are indicated by flatting the respective pitches. Thus, in the key of C, the E, G, and B would be replaced by E♭, G♭, and B♭. Sometimes the E♮ and the blue note (E♭) are struck simultaneously on the piano, creating the characteristic sound of blues. From the combination of blue notes and the scale notes of C major an artificial *blues scale* can be created.

By omitting one note of this scale, we derive a second version of the blues scale.

This scale consists of six notes and has only one more note (G♭) than the minor tonal pentatonic scale. It is frequently used in blues performances, especially in descending from the high C to the low C.

The next exercise deals with these special scales: the whole tone, the pentatonic, and the blues scales.

19

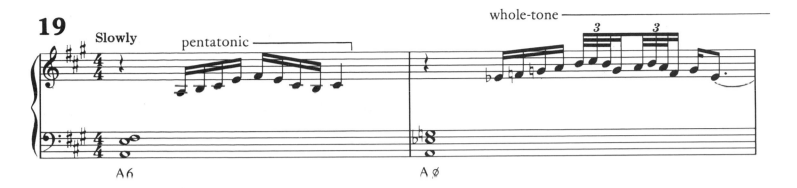

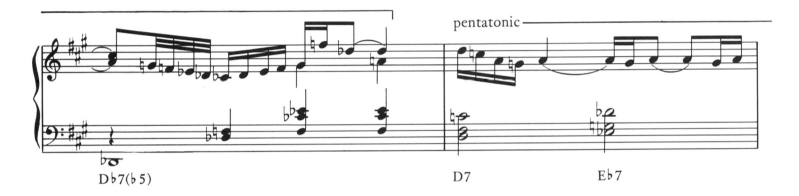

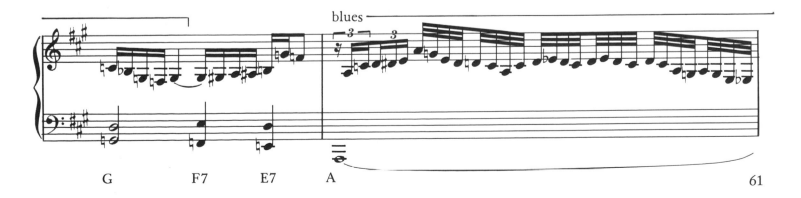

62

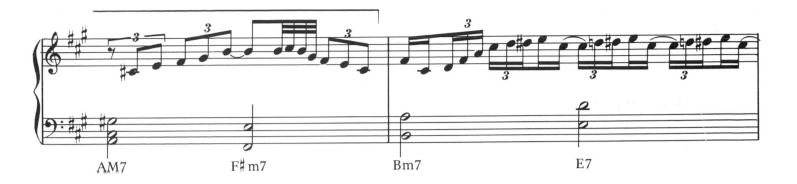

AM7   F#m7   Bm7   E7

pentatonic

A6   D7   C7   Bb7

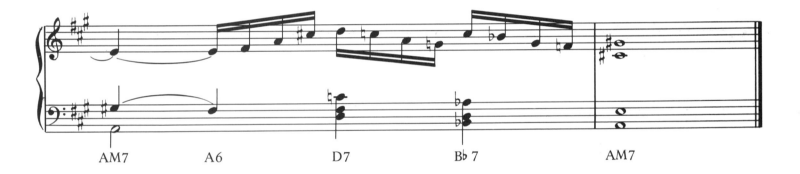

AM7   A6   D7   Bb7   AM7

Swing Piano Style

The swing era of the 30s and 40s is considered by many as the golden age of jazz pianism. It grew from the ashes of the dying ragtime of the 20s and faded out in the late 40s with the dawn of the modern bebop movement. Among the hundreds of piano soloists of the swing era we must mention the names of the great innovators who forged the style of jazz piano: Teddy Wilson, Art Tatum, "Fats" Waller, Earl Hines, Bud Powell, and George Shearing.

The left-hand technique of the so-called "stride" piano consists of a deep bass single note struck with the fifth finger, and a chord situated around the middle C of the piano, played with four fingers. The following two exercises are devoted to this left-hand technique exclusively. In the first exercise, the fifth finger strikes a single note on the first and third beats of the measure; in the second exercise this single note is replaced by a tenth or a chord. The second and fourth beats (the afterbeats) consist of chords. Inversions of chords are preferable to root positions. It is recommended to place the third or the fifth of the chord on the top. The latter voicing is especially suitable for minor sevenths and half-diminished seventh chords. The diminished chord can be used in any inversion.

C6   Cm6   C7   Cm7   C ø   C o   or   C o

The same chord on the afterbeats can be used with different bass notes played with the fifth finger on the first and third beats of the measure.

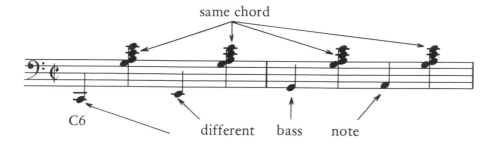

The above rules are not absolute. The student should use his judgment in determining which inversion is the most suitable and sounds best in the given context.

20

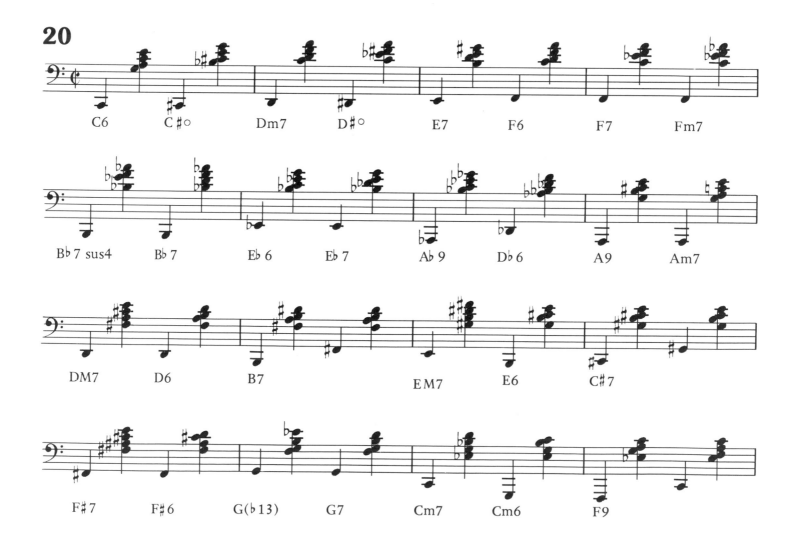

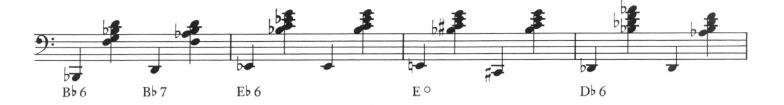

Bb 6   Bb 7   Eb 6   E °   Db 6

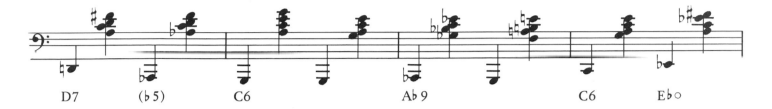

D7   (b5)   C6   Ab 9   C6   Eb°

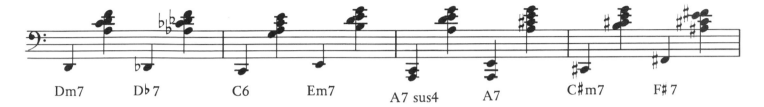

Dm7   Db 7   C6   Em7   A7 sus4   A7   C#m7   F# 7

Bm7   E7   Em7   A7   Dm7   G7   CM7(9)   C6

Bass Tenth System

Another important left-hand technique used during the swing era was the bass tenth system. The characteristic feature of this system is the replacement of the single bass note by a tenth. This interval can be easy, difficult, or impossible to play, depending on the reach of the student's hand and on the position of the tenth on the keyboard.

easy   difficult   very difficult
                          or impossible

The bass tenth has a twofold function: as a substitute for a single note, or as a substitute for a whole chord. The following example shows the substitution of a tenth for all kinds of chords.

GM7   G7   Gm7   G ø   G °   Gm6

The monotony of an "oom-pah" accompaniment could be avoided by replacing some of the chords on the second and fourth beats with tenths, thus creating a more interesting and varied bass line. Here are some consecutive tenths, moving in a diatonic, chromatic, or mixed motion.

The left-hand swing system can be enriched by the addition of whole chords. Many of these chords will be beyond the reach of the student, but the use of only a few will considerably vary the bass line. To create even more diversity, the tenths and seventh chords could alternate with simple triads and short melodic phrases.

21

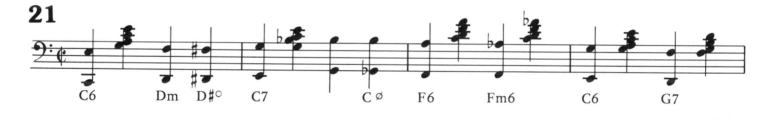

66

Cm6   F9   B♭   F   B♭   Dø

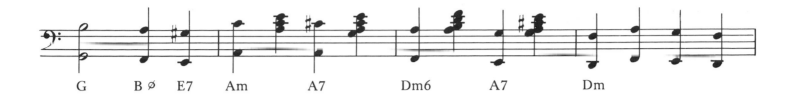

G   Bø   E7   Am   A7   Dm6   A7   Dm

Gm7   C7   F   F   C7   E♭o   G7   C6   Dm   D♯o   C7   Cø

F6   Fm6   C6   G7   C6   F6   C6   G7   C

22

C6   C♯o   Dm   Em7   Am7

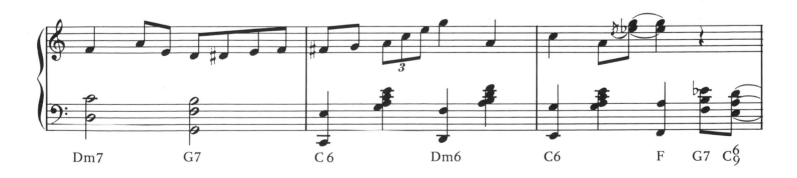

Dm7   G7   C6   Dm6   C6   F   G7   C$^6_9$

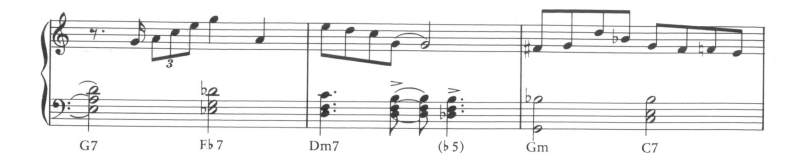

G7   F♭7   Dm7   (♭5)   Gm   C7

Gm   C7   F6   C7   F6   F7

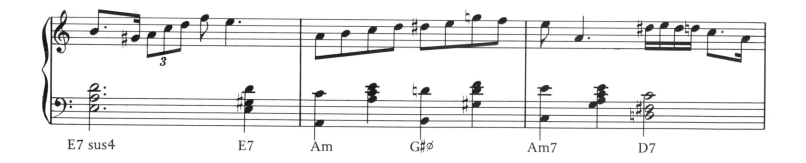

B♭m   E♭11   D9   D♭7(♯5)   C7   C(♯11)

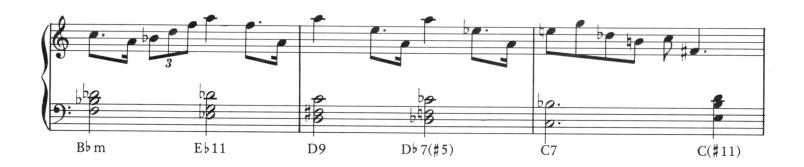

E7 sus4   E7   Am   G♯ø   Am7   D7

Am   E7   Am   B7

Em7   A7   D7   G   G#°

A7   D7   C7   Bb 7   Ab 7

G7   C7(b5)   F6   C7

F7   Bb 6   F   C7   F   G7

C6   G7   C6   F6   E7   A7

Bebop Piano Style

The mid-forties can be considered a turning point in the history of jazz, one which has had a profound influence on all succeeding generations of jazz musicians. Four great innovators can be credited for this new revolutionary movement: Charlie Parker, Dizzy Gillespie, Miles Davis, and Art Tatum.

The name bebop is probably derived from the nonsensical syllables "rebop" and "be-bop" which were sometimes sung over short rhythmical phrases. The new music contained so many harmonic, melodic, and rhythmic innovations that it created enormous breaches not only among musicians themselves, but also between the musicians and their audiences.

It is not within the scope of this book to analyze in detail all the features of bebop. Suffice it to mention some of its prominent characteristics, the most important of which is the harmonic language. Whereas the harmony of traditional jazz is diatonic, much of the new vocabulary was based on chromaticicm. Bebop made extensive use of altered notes (especially the flatted fifth), passing notes, substitute chords, eleventh and thir-teenth chords, modal and whole-tone scales, etc.

The main rhythmic innovation consisted of the replacing of the steady four-beats-to-the-bar with rhythmic punctuations and syncopations occurring at irregular time inter-vals, on any subdivision of the meter. The feeling of rhythmic security was further dis-turbed by the increased use of double time, in which irregular accents on eighth and sixteenth notes gave the impression of twice as many bars as actually played.

Jazz composers before the bebop era usually strove for smooth melodic lines built of regular 2- and 4-bar phrases, which created the sensation of predictability and inevitabi-lity. The bop melodic line is irregular, consisting of snatches of phrases, discontinued melodies, large skips, and unusual intervals. This lack of tunefulness, as well as the disso-nant harmonies and the rhythmic complexity, created the gap between the bop musician and his listener, which was further widened by the protagonists of "progressive" jazz.

23

F+(♯9)   F(♭9)♭5   E(♯9)   C(♯9) B9   B♭9

C(♯11)   G♭11   F(♭9)♭5   E♭7   D7 sus4

G(♯9)13 C(♯9) B(♯9)   B♭M7   Cm7   F7   E♭M7

Fm7   B♭9   A9 A♭9 G9   G♭(♯11)

F9   C(♭9)♭5   G♭(♯9)   F9   E(♯9)   E♭7

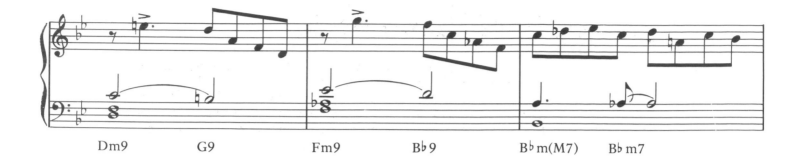

Dm9   G9   Fm9   Bb9   Bbm(M7)   Bbm7

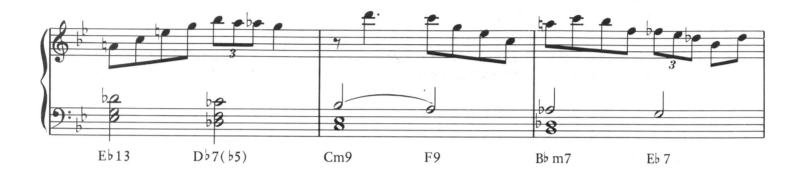

Eb13   Db7(b5)   Cm9   F9   Bbm7   Eb7

AbM7   Ab6   G7   Gb9   F+(#9)   F(b9)b5

E(#9)   C(#9)   B9   Bb6/9   C(#11)   Gb11   F(b9)b5

Eb7   D7sus4   G(#9)13 B(b13) Bb13

Block Chord Piano Style

This piano style is intrinsically connected with the name of George Shearing, who developed it toward the end of the 1940s. As the name implies, the melodic line does not consist of single notes but of block chords similar to the woodwind section of Glenn Miller's band. The technique of this style is simple: the melody moves in parallel octaves, the space between the octave notes being filled with three inner voices. For instance, the motive

would be played in five-note chords, the right hand playing the top voice and the three inner voices, the left hand playing the bottom octave note of the melody.

As you can see from the above example, the essential notes of the C-major triad (C E G) are present in each chord, plus the added sixth or seventh. It is important to remember that the essential quality of each chord should be retained, *i.e.* the notes which determine the quality of the chord should appear in the block chords.

It is also possible to add a bass note to the block chords, playing it with the fifth finger of the left hand.

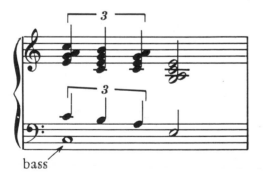

bass

24

C6   CM7   C6   Dm7   D♭9   C6   C°

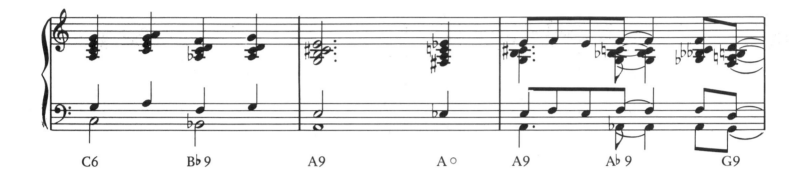

C6   B♭9   A9   A°   A9   A♭9   G9

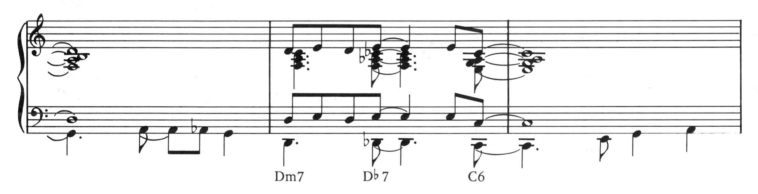

Dm7   D♭7   C6

B♭9   B♭9   B♭(♭9)   E7   E♭6   A♭9

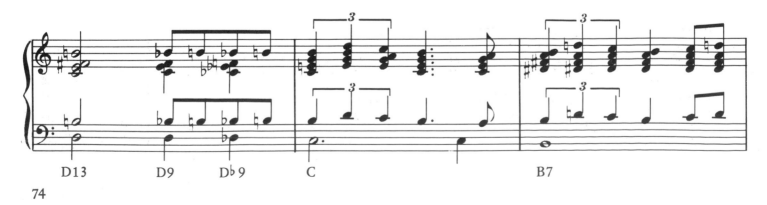

D13   D9   D♭9   C   B7

E7   A9   Am7

D9   Ab 9   GM7   Gm6

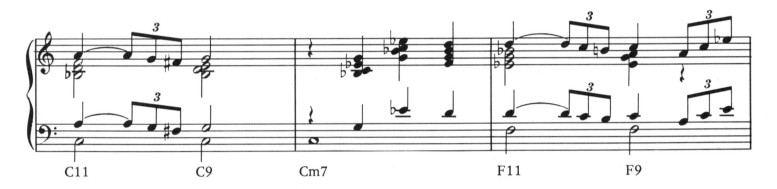

C11   C9   Cm7   F11   F9

Bb 11   Bb 9   Ab 11   Ab 9   G7   Ab 7   G7

Cm6   F9   CM7   C6   Cm7   C6/9

Modern Voicing

"Voicing" means an arrangement of the notes of a chord in a special way so as to create an unusual sound. This is achieved by omitting certain chord components (usually the root) and emphasizing other chord members.

There are no simple rules for doing this. The student is advised to experiment with the unlimited possibilities of chord inversions and alterations. It is obvious that the essential notes should not be omitted. For instance, the seventh in a seventh chord should always be present as well as the third, which determines if the chord is major or minor. As explained before, the missing notes can be supplied by the right hand for a fuller voicing. When accompanying a singer ("comping") or another musician, the chords can be played with both hands. Modern pianists avoid playing them *on* the beat; a syncopated chordal accompaniment is essential for creating the unusual contemporary sound heard in recent jazz and rock recordings.

A left-hand voicing can consist of only two notes and still give the impression of a full chord. Playing only the F and B can suggest the dominant seventh chord of C major.

More complicated chord structures require more notes, but here also good taste and the melodic line will determine the voicing.

We have familiarized ourselves with the most common progression in music, the II-V-I progression. A great number of voicings can be applied to this progression because it contains all kinds of seventh chords, especially the dominant seventh chord with its numerous alterations and substitutions. Here are some voicings for the I, II, and V chords in C major and minor.

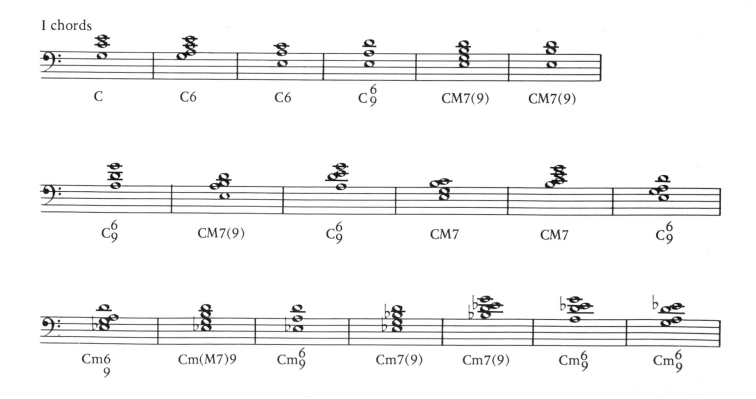

Chord Symbol Appendix

C major with added sixth	C6
C major seventh	CM7, or Cmaj 7, or C△
C major with added sixth and ninth	C$^6_9$
C minor	Cm
C minor seventh	Cm7
C minor with added sixth	Cm6
C minor with added major seventh	Cm(M7)
C dominant seventh	C7
C dominant ninth	C9
C dominant flat ninth	C(♭9)
C eleventh	C11
C augmented eleventh	C(♯11)
C thirteenth	C13
C flat thirteenth	C(♭13)
C half-diminished seventh	C⌀, or Cm7(♭5)
C diminished seventh	C°, or Cdim, or Cdim7
C augmented triad	C+, or C+5, or C♯5
C dominant seventh with flat fifth	C7(♭5)
C dominant seventh with augmented fifth	C+7, or C7(♯5)
C suspended fourth	Csus, or C(sus4)
C major with F bass	C/F
C ninth without the third	C9 omit3